KUEST:Rocket
Character Series

I0168923

STUDENT
JOURNAL

©2019 Current Family, Inc.
www.KUEST.org
All Rights Reserved
First printing 2011

ISBN-13: 978-1-950616-05-3

EXCELLENCE - TEAMWORK - AUTHORITY

KUEST KODE:

1 Timothy 4:12 (NLT)

"Don't let anyone think less of you because you are young. Be an example to all believers in what you say, in the way you live, in your love, your faith, and your purity."

Be the BEST you!

Being a **KUEST Kid** is all about giving your absolute best in everything you do! As you go through this journal, you will be learning valuable lessons about **Excellence, Teamwork** and **Authority**. How much you learn and how much these lessons help you get stronger is up to you! Take the time to read every scripture and every lesson and do the exercise and your spirit will get stronger and stronger. A strong spirit will help you make great choices and live the best life! Welcome to **KUEST Student Leadership!**

KUEST™

Student Leadership

This journal belongs to:

_____

I am a KUEST Leader!

1.1 EXCELLENCE

Excellence is an Attitude

attitude
an attitude is a way of thinking about someone or something

Jeremiah 29:11

"For I know the thoughts that I think towards you, says the LORD, thoughts of peace and not of evil, to give you a future and a hope."

Learning to be excellent will set you up for a **GREAT LIFE!** Learning to be excellent means learning to give your best **EVERY TIME** you have a job to do, a class to take, a chore to do, a speech to give, and so on. It means learning to think like a **CHAMPION!** And it means learning to think differently than some of your friends.

Sometimes being excellent means doing extra work. Sometimes it means staying a little later. Sometimes it means starting over. But it will always mean that you can say, **"I did the absolute best I could do."** And the number one way to be able to say that everytime you do anything is to have an excellent attitude!

Here is a KUESTion:

What are some things you **think** **God** thinks about **you**?

Write your answer here:

"An **ATTITUDE** is a way of thinking that becomes a way of life. Make **EXCELLENCE** your way of thinking!"

2

HOW DO YOU FEEL? Circle how the statement makes you feel.
Then ask yourself, "What can I do to improve my attitude about that?"

	happy, excited	whatever	sad, afraid, mad, bored
1. Cleaning your room:	☺	😐	☹
2. Taking out the trash:	☺	😐	☹
3. Playing video games:	☺	😐	☹
4. Talking on the phone:	☺	😐	☹
5. Doing homework:	☺	😐	☹
6. Eating Pizza:	☺	😐	☹
7. Reading your bible:	☺	😐	☹
8. Obeying your parents:	☺	😐	☹

HOW DO YOUR FRIENDS FEEL? Ask a friend to complete the
same exercise, then compare the differences.

	happy, excited	whatever	sad, afraid, mad, bored
1. Cleaning your room:	☺	😐	☹
2. Taking out the trash:	☺	😐	☹
3. Playing video games:	☺	😐	☹
4. Talking on the phone:	☺	😐	☹
5. Doing homework:	☺	😐	☹
6. Eating Pizza:	☺	😐	☹
7. Reading your bible:	☺	😐	☹
8. Obeying your parents:	☺	😐	☹

Journal Minute

Today's Date: / /

How was your day today?

What was something funny that happened?

What was something bad that happened?

What did you learn from this lesson?

attitude

an attitude is a way of thinking about someone or something

Galatians 6:3

"For if anyone thinks he is something when he is really nothing, he is only fooling himself."

Have you ever been afraid to try something? A friend says, **"Here, stick your hand in this bag!"** You are not sure what is in the bag, and the look on your friend's face makes you **THINK** that they want to trick you. What would you do?

The answer is different for each of us because our answers are based on what we think. If you think there is nothing in the bag that can hurt you, then you will reach right in. If you think there is something in the bag that WILL hurt you, then a thousand ninjas could not make you put your hand in that bag! What we **THINK** determines the way we **ACT**!

Here is a KUESTion:

What do you **think about** the most every day?

Write your answer here:

The way we THINK determines the way we ACT!

WHO ARE YOU? Write a description of yourself. Write down the things you like to do and don't like to do. Write down how you act or what you are good at:

I really like to:

I don't like to:

Sometimes I act:

I am really good at:

Journal Minute

Today's Date: / /

How was your day today?

What was something funny that happened?

What was something bad that happened?

What did you learn from this lesson?

Excellence is an Attitude

attitude

an attitude is a way of thinking about someone or something

Romans 12:2

"Don't copy the behavior and customs of this world, but let God transform you into a new person by changing the way you think."

Did you know that you can actually change the way you think about something? Learning to get rid of bad attitudes and replace them with good attitudes will help you be excellent and successful in life. People with **BAD ATTITUDES** hardly ever get promotions and raises on the job. People with **GOOD ATTITUDES** are usually the ones who become leaders and receive bonuses.

Kids who have bad attitudes usually spend alot of time in the Principal's office. Kids with good attitudes usually get better grades and have more privileges. A good attitude is worth having, a bad attitude is worth nothing. But good and bad attitudes are just attitudes; to be excellent, we have to choose the **RIGHT** attitude.

Here is a KUESTion:

Have **you** ever made a good **choice?** What happened?

Write your answer here:

GOOD ATTITUDES and bad attitudes are just attitudes. To be excellent we must choose the **RIGHT attitude.**

Change Your Attitude = Change Your Action: Draw a line from the bad attitude to the bad action. Then draw a line from the bad action to the good attitude, then from the good attitude to the good action.

BAD ATTITUDES

School is boring

I can do it later

that's good enough

this isn't fun

this isn't fair

he is weird

BAD ACTIONS

whining & complaining

skip homework

never get it done

making fun of others

sloppy work

treating others meanly

GOOD ATTITUDES

do it now

I can do better

I love helping

I'm glad for others

I will be his friend

I love to learn

GOOD ACTIONS

work hard in class

never wait to get stuff done

let others go first

be a good friend

be excellent

being a great helper

Journal Minute

Today's Date: [/ /]

How was your day today?

What was something funny that happened?

What was something bad that happened?

What did you learn from this lesson?

attitude

an attitude is a way of thinking about someone or something

James 4:17

"Anyone, then, who knows the good he ought to do and doesn't do it, sins."

Sometimes we know what we **SHOULD** do, but we choose to not do it because we think what we **WANT** to do is better. Sometimes we know what we **SHOULD** do, but we choose to not do it because we think nothing bad will happen if we don't. Like, we show up late for class because we don't think the teacher will mark us down as tardy. Or we take another cookie, even though mom said, "no", because we don't think she will find out.

Sometimes we don't understand **WHY** we should do the right thing, or we forget **WHY** we should do the right thing, and so we end up doing the wrong thing. Is that **RIGHT** thinking or **WRONG** thinking?

Here is a KUESTion:

Why do you think it is important for us to make
GOOD CHOICES?

Write your answer here:

When you know **WHY** you will give it a **TRY**!

Knowing why you should or should not do something will help you make good choices. Draw a line from the items under **SHOULD** and **SHOULD NOT** to the why.

SHOULD

obey your parents

do your best

pray for others

SHOULD NOT

make fun of others

cheat at school

skip church

be late

WHY

it is selfish and hurts the team

miss a chance to learn more about Jesus

hurtS other's feelings

encourages their spirit

you will only get in trouble

God honors you

helps you improve

Journal Minute

Today's Date: / /

How was your day today?

What was something funny that happened?

What was something bad that happened?

What did you learn from this lesson?

It's Not About Me!

Teamwork means making the team more important than me!

Philippians 2:4

"Each of you should look not only to your own interests, but also to the interests of others."

Did you know that soon after Jesus left Earth and went back to Heaven, that the disciples started telling others about Jesus and that the number of people who believed got bigger and bigger? Because so many people started believing in Jesus, they started to form churches and started to look out for each other. In fact, the Bible says that nobody ever had any needs that weren't met because everyone took care of each other.

What would it be like if everybody just looked out for each other? If you made sure everyone had what they needed, and they were making sure everyone had what they needed, then everyone would have what they need. Learning to look out for each other will make your team stronger than ever!

Here is a KUESTion:

How can you help **look out** for others on your **team?**

Write your answer here:

"Look **OUT** for your team!"

18

SEEING SPOTS? Learning to pay attention is one way to learn how to look out for others. Practice paying attention by counting how many circles are in the space below? Too easy? Count how many "i"'s are on the two pages of this lesson!

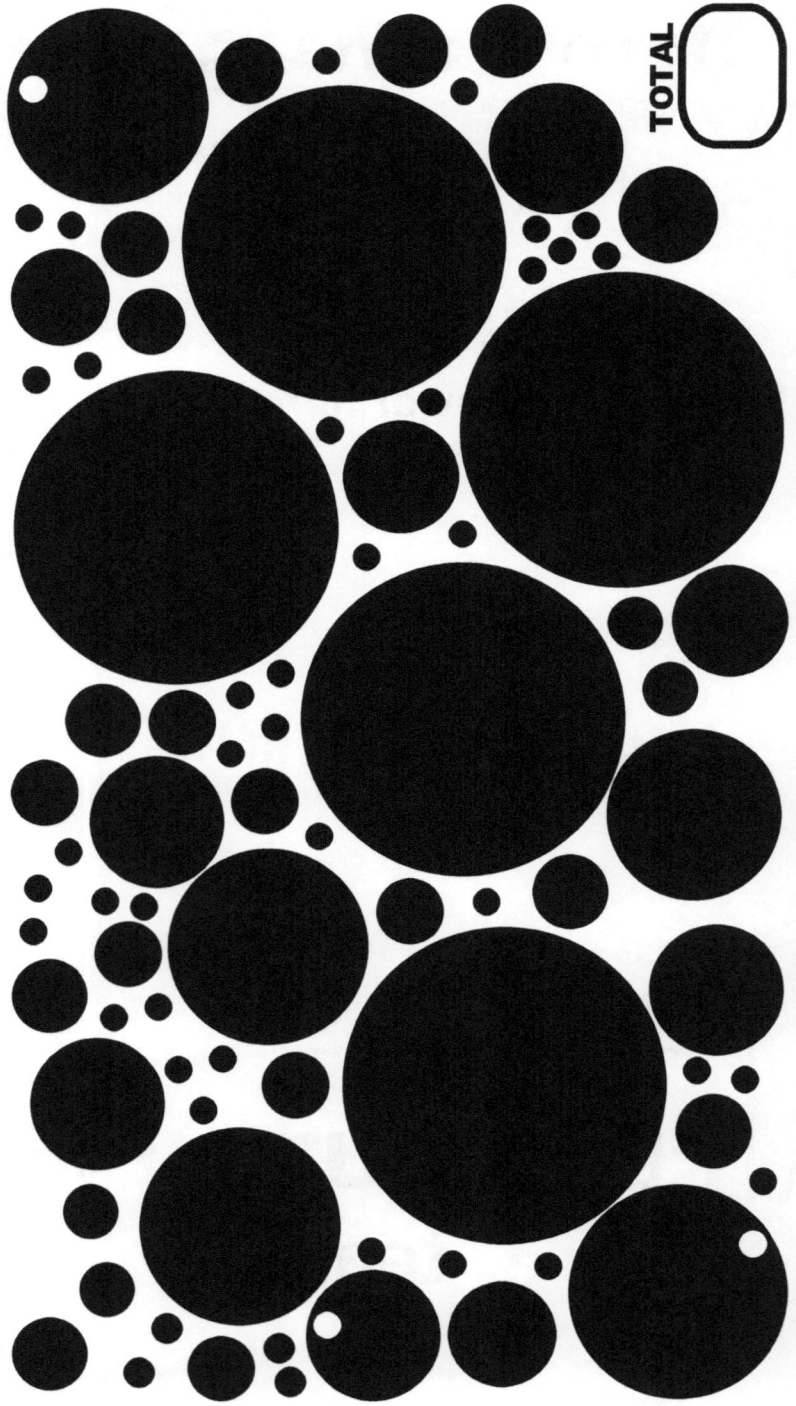

TOTAL

Journal Minute

Today's Date: | / / |

How was your day today?

What was something funny that happened?

What was something bad that happened?

What did you learn from this lesson?

It's Not About Me!

Teamwork means making the team more important than me!

Mark 2:3-4

"Four men arrived carrying a paralyzed man on a mat. They couldn't bring him to Jesus because of the crowd, so they dug a hole through the roof above his head. Then they lowered the man on his mat, right down in front of Jesus. "

The story above is some serious teamwork! These guys did not have matching jerseys, or a locker room. They did not have a team handshake or a secret code for getting into their secret hideout. They were a team because they had one common goal, to help their friend get healed. Sometimes people work together simply because there is something that needs to be done. When you work with other people to get a job done, work is much easier, you get stuff done much faster. But the bottom line is, when you have the chance to serve on any team, you have to forget about you and give your best to the team!

Here is a KUESTion:

Have you ever done something AMAZING for a friend?

Write your answer here:

Nothing GREAT has ever been done without a TEAM!

WHAT DO THEY DO? Draw a line from the team to what the team does:

Baseball team   Plays Music

Firefighter team   Are related

Dance Team   Builds houses

Family   Puts on a show

High school band   Puts out fires

Construction crew   Plays a sport

IT'S A DRAW: Pick a team from the list above and draw a picture of them below.

Journal Minute

Today's Date: | / / |

How was your day today?

What was something funny that happened?

What was something bad that happened?

What did you learn from this lesson?

It's Not About Me!

Teamwork means making the team more important than me!

Philippians 2:3

"Don't push your way to the front; don't sweet-talk your way to the top. Put yourself aside, and help others get ahead. "

Have you ever been to the zoo? What happens when an animal is being especially active and doing funny stuff? People gather around to watch and what do most people do? They push their way to the front of the crowd so they can get to see what the animal is doing. This is especially true for smaller kids because they cannot see over or around most adults. Once they get to the front, all they are thinking about is watching the animal and not at all about if other kids need a turn. What would be the KUEST Kid thing to do? How about taking your turn, and then helping someone else get a good look? This is the picture Philippians 2:3 is showing us. All of us working together for the good of each other. When you are working on a team, it is important that you ignore your options and choices and stay focused on the goal of the team.

Here is a KUESTion:

Have you ever let someone else go **first**? What happened?

Write your answer here:

The **GREATNESS** of your **TEAM** is your **CHOICE!**

I'M PUZZLED: Number the pieces to the left to match where they belong on the right. Then redraw their images in the numbered squares to the right to complete the picture. We gave you a start with #5. Feel free to color the picture when you're done!

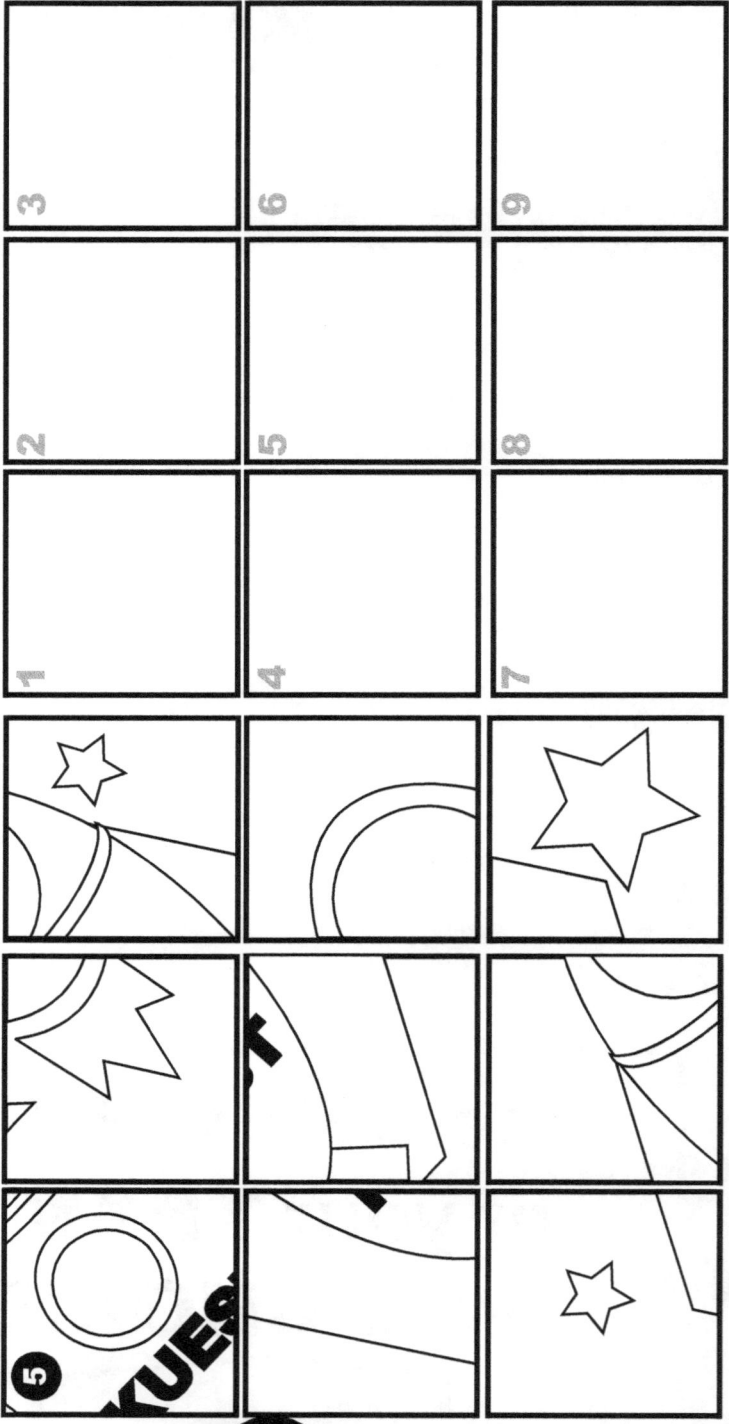

Journal Minute

Today's Date: | / / |

How was your day today?

What was something funny that happened?

What was something bad that happened?

What did you learn from this lesson?

It's Not About Me!

Teamwork means making the team more important than me!

---

1 Thessalonians 5:11

(AMP) - "Therefore encourage (admonish, exhort) one another and edify (strengthen and build up) one another..."

Here are some **STRANGE** words for you: Admonish and Exhort **ADMONISH/EXHORT** = to urge to a duty. So we are to urge and remind each other to keep working hard, keep getting the job done, and we are supposed to **BUILD** each other up! This is such a great picture of being on a team. Not only are we cheering each other on, but we are also doing whatever we have to do to help each other succeed. This is exactly what it means to work together as a team!

This is what it is like to be a strong, healthy team that gets stuff done. We realize that it is "Not about me!" We **LOOK OUT** for each other. We forget about our options and do our part, and we put our full strength behind helping others be their best! That is **TEAMWORK!**

Here is a KUESTion:

Have you ever used your words to **ENCOURAGE** someone?

Write your answer here:

Tell your team, "I **AM HERE FOR YOU!**"

30

HERE TO HELP: Choose five of your friends for the jobs below. Then ask them what they could do in that role to help the others do their job even better. For instance, your puppet person might help the singer learn to memorize the songs.

JOB	PERSON
1. **Lead Singer**	_____
2. **Cleanup Crew**	_____
3. **Puppets**	_____
4. **Prop Maker**	_____
5. **Actor/Actress**	_____

WHAT DO THEY NEED? Draw a picture of the tools that each of the above team members might use. For instance, for the cleanup crew, you might draw a broom.

Journal Minute

Today's Date:

/	/

How was your day today?

What was something funny that happened?

What was something bad that happened?

What did you learn from this lesson?

God is my Authority

Recognizing Authority

All authority comes from God!

---

1 Kings 18:44

"Finally the seventh time, his servant told him, 'I saw a little cloud about the size of a man's hand rising from the sea.' Then Elijah shouted, 'Hurry to Ahab and tell him, Climb into your chariot and go back home. If you don't hurry, the rain will stop you!'"

Elijah was expecting to see a sign from God that there was going to be rain. He told his servant to go look for a sign, and six times his servant saw nothing. Finally, on the seventh time he saw a small cloud. That cloud had authority with it. Elijah's servant wasn't sure if it was that important, but Elijah recognized the sign and the authority. He recognized that God was about to send rain and it was going to be a downpour. There are signs of authority all around us, we just have to learn to recognize them.

Here is a KUESTion:

Have you ever seen a **HUGE** cloud? What did you think?

Write your answer here:

Authority is the POWER to RULE!

IT'S A SIGN: Here are some unique signs. Draw a line from the sign to their possible meaning. Some of the signs could mean more than one thing, so choose wisely.

Severe Weather

Parking

wait here

Airport

Bus Stop

Campground

Restaurant

DANGER: High Voltage

Poison

Public Telephone

Bike Path

Journal Minute

Today's Date: | / / |

How was your day today?

What was something funny that happened?

What was something bad that happened?

What did you learn from this lesson?

God is my Authority

Recognizing Authority

All authority comes from God!

Genesis 3:11-12

11 ...the LORD God asked. "Have you eaten from the tree whose fruit I commanded you not to eat?" 12 The man replied, "It was the woman you gave me who gave me the fruit, and I ate it."

Adam and Eve were **BUSTED!** They got caught doing something they should not have done. Even though God had told them they should not eat of that tree, they did. Adam and Eve did not recognize the authority of God's Rules. They might have thought they got away with it, but they did not. Laws are laws and rules are rules. Laws and rules do not change for one person or the next, they are the same for everyone. Gravity is an example of a law that works the same way for everyone. If you walk off the edge of a **HIGH CLIFF**, you will fall to the ground below. That works exactly the same way for everyone. All of us must recognize the laws and authority around us and learn to obey those laws and authority.

Here is a KUESTion:

Have you ever broken a
RULE? What happened?

Write your answer here:

All **authority** is given by **GOD!**

EGG ON YOUR FACE: Use the space below to practice drawing your face on an egg. Then get two real eggs, and make them look like you. With your parent's help, drop one egg into their hands. Did it break? Now have them hold rocks in their hands while you drop another egg. Did that one break? The authority of gravity works the same for everyone, and recognizing authority will help us be our best!

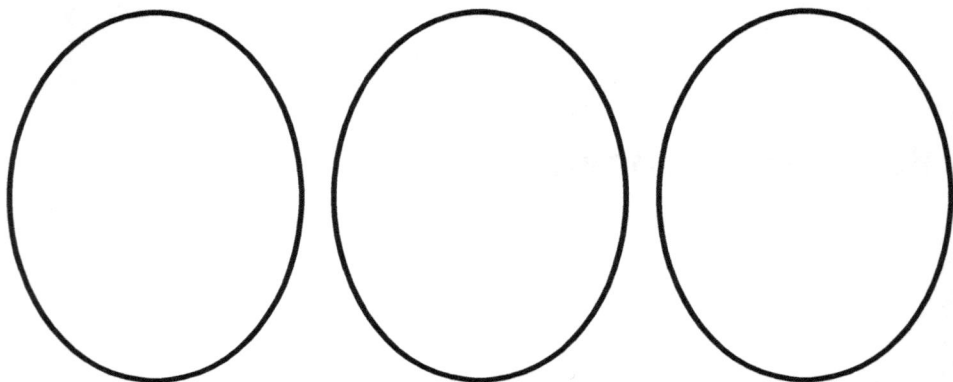

DECORATE! Decorate this egg with amazing designs and colors! Get creative!!

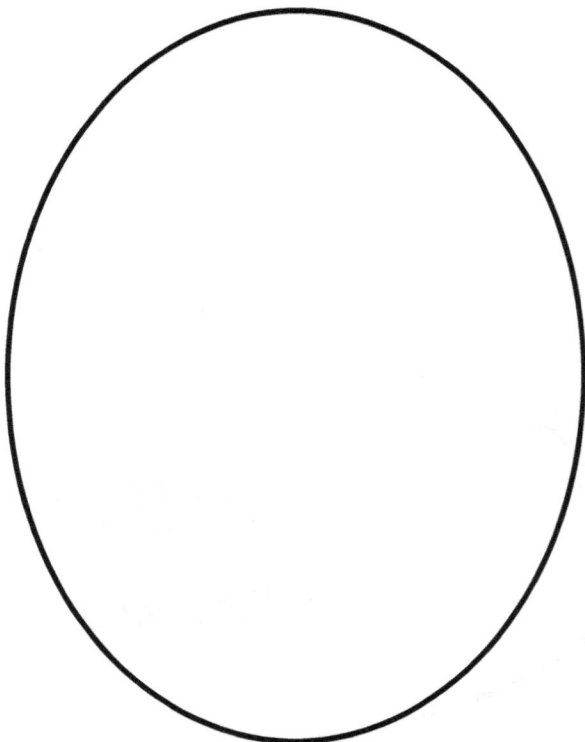

Journal Minute

Today's Date: | / / |

How was your day today?

What was something funny that happened?

What was something bad that happened?

What did you learn from this lesson?

God is my Authority

Recognizing Authority

All authority comes from God!

---

1 Kings 19:12

"And after the earthquake there was a fire, but the LORD was not in the fire. And after the fire there was the sound of a gentle whisper."

Elijah had one of those moments where he thought he heard something he didn't actually hear. Like when you thought you heard thunder, but it was actually just a loud car going by. Learning to recognize what we see and hear helps us avoid danger and find safety. Learning to recognize authority will help you enjoy success in life. Did you know that learning to recognize the authority of your parents is one of the ways God teaches us to stay safe and be successful in life?

Even when you are busy, and have a lot going on, you have to learn to recognize signs of authority. Use your ears, listen for what God is saying, learn to tune out distractions and listen for the voice of authority. Even if you're watching TV, learn to hear your parents when they call, that is learning to recognize authority.

Here is a KUESTion:

Have you ever seen a **HUGE** cloud? What did you think?

Write your answer here:

Authority is all
AROUND US!

LISTEN CLOSELY: Turn on your favorite kids TV show, close your eyes and listen. Write down seven sounds or phrases and who made the sounds or said the phrases.

SOUND #1: _____ _____

SOUND #2: _____ _____

SOUND #3: _____ _____

SOUND #4: _____ _____

SOUND #5: _____ _____

SOUND #6: _____ _____

SOUND #7: _____ _____

LISTEN CLOSER: Now go outside, sit on your porch and close your eyes. Write down at least 7 sounds and what made the sounds.

SOUND #1: _____ _____

SOUND #2: _____ _____

SOUND #3: _____ _____

SOUND #4: _____ _____

SOUND #5: _____ _____

SOUND #6: _____ _____

SOUND #7: _____ _____

Journal Minute

Today's Date: | / / |

How was your day today?

What was something funny that happened?

What was something bad that happened?

What did you learn from this lesson?

God is my Authority

Recognizing Authority

All authority comes from God!

John 14:26

"But the Counselor, the Holy Spirit, whom the Father will send in my name, will teach you all things and will remind you of everything I have said to you."

Jesus said that the Holy Spirit would help his disciples to remember everything that He had taught them. He said that the Holy Spirit would **RE-MIND** them. But the only way to be RE-minded, is if you were **MINDED** in the first place. The only reason you can remember where you went on vacation is because you went there. The only reason you can remember what you had for lunch is because you ate it. So what is the only way you can remember what someone said? The only reason you can remember what someone said is because you heard them say it in the first place. The Holy Spirit will help us remember what has been said to us to help us be our best. So remember to pay attention to what is being said by those in authority over you. Recognize, respect and respond to authority for the best life.

Here is a KUESTion:

Have you ever remembered something **IMPORTANT?**

Write your answer here:

Looking back helps you **MOVE FORWARD!**

THE LIST: On another sheet of paper, have someone make a list of numbers, a list of names and a list of colors. Have them let you see each list one at a time for about 30 seconds. Then write down as much as you can remember from their list in the spaces below.

NAMES	NUMBERS	COLORS
_____	_____	_____
_____	_____	_____
_____	_____	_____
_____	_____	_____
_____	_____	_____
_____	_____	_____
_____	_____	_____
_____	_____	_____
_____	_____	_____

Journal Minute

Today's Date: | / / |

How was your day today?

What was something funny that happened?

What was something bad that happened?

What did you learn from this lesson?

Expectation

Learn to raise your level of self expectation.

Genesis 1:25

"And God made the beast of the earth according to its kind, cattle according to its kind, and everything that creeps on the earth according to its kind. And God saw that it was good. "

When God was creating the universe, there wasn't anybody looking over His shoulder telling Him what to do and how to do it. All the excellence that God put into the whole earth, every animal, every bird, every fish and even you and me came from His own Spirit. God created everything from His own expectation of excellence. What if God would have decided to not do His best in creating the World? What if He would have thought, "Nobody is watching me, so I'm gonna just hurry up and get this done, who cares about how good it is!" That would have been bad! What might have been different if God did not expect excellence of Himself? God created us to be excellent but we have to put our best into everything we do!

Here is a KUESTion:

Have you ever **NOT GIVEN** your absolute **BEST?**

Write your answer here:

Expect MORE from YOURSELF!

EXCELLENCE TEST: Have a friend time you as you learn to combine speed with excellence. Follow the instructions for each star. Next to each star, write down how long it took you to color that star. Then compare how excellently you colored each one.

Color this star as neatly as you can!

Color this star as neatly and quickly as you can!

Color this star as quickly as you can!

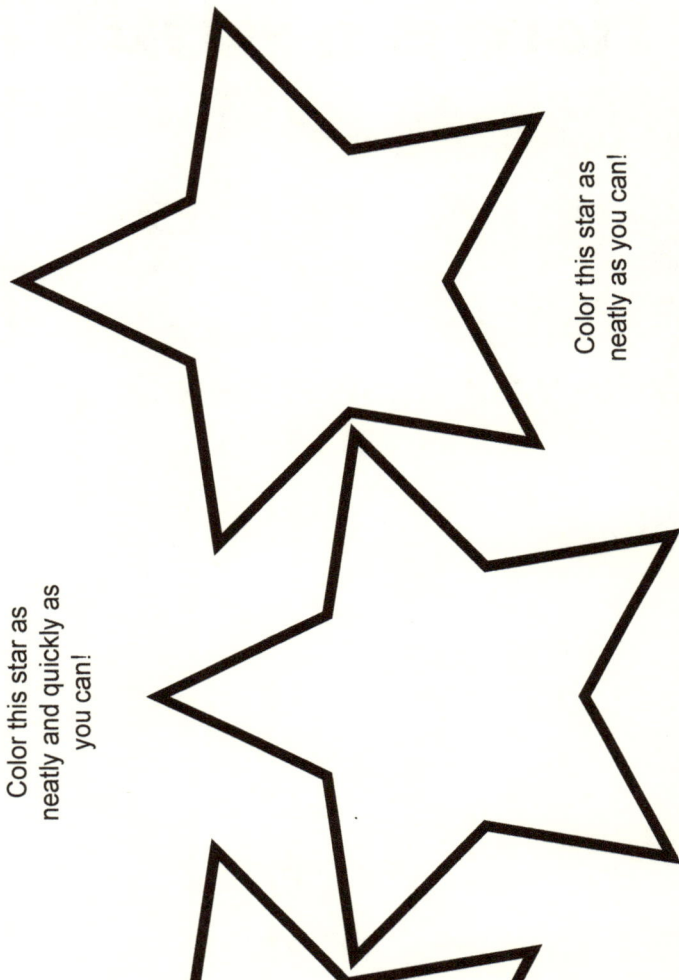

Journal Minute

Today's Date: _____ / _____ / _____

How was your day today?

What was something funny that happened?

What was something bad that happened?

What did you learn from this lesson?

Excellence is an Attitude

Expectation

Learn to raise your level of self expectation.

Luke 10:33-34

"But a certain Samaritan, as he journeyed, came where he was. And when he saw him, he had compassion. So he went to him and bandaged his wounds, pouring on oil and wine; and he set him on his own animal, brought him to an inn, and took care of him."

Several people, even a priest, had walked by this guy who was laying on the ground. Even though they saw his wounds and knew he needed help, they just walked around him and never helped. Except for this one Samaritan who decided to be excellent and compassionate, even when everybody else was not. Sometimes, to be excellent, we have to do what nobody else will do. We have to travel down a road where no one else will go. We have to reach out to people that no one else will reach out to. Raising your level of excellence means expecting more from yourself even when no one else will do the job!

Here is a KUESTion:

Have you ever CHOSEN to be excellent, even when others were not?

Write your answer here:

Be EXCELLENT even when OTHERS are not!

GOOD, BAD & UGLY: Find four objects and rate their condition. After you have rated the objects, think about what you would do to make the objects even more excellent.

	YUCK	BAD	ALRIGHT	EXCELLENT
OBJECT 1				
OBJECT 2				
OBJECT 3				
OBJECT 4				

Journal Minute

Today's Date: | / / |

How was your day today?

What was something funny that happened?

What was something bad that happened?

What did you learn from this lesson?

Expectation

Learn to raise your level of self expectation.

1 Corinthians 12:31

"But earnestly desire the best gifts."

EARNESTLY = serious in intention, purpose, or effort; intense
DESIRE = crave or ask for

EARNESTLY DESIRE = to crave intensely!

Have you every wanted something so badly that you could hardly stand it? Did you know that God wants you to **EARNESTLY DESIRE** (crave intensely) the best gifts He has for you? He wants you to want His gifts so badly that you can hardly stand it! One of God's gifts is excellence. God wants you to want to be excellent so bad that you can hardly stand it! Have you ever stood in a store and tried to decide which toy, or jewelry or game you were going to buy? What is the longest you have ever taken to make a decision? Why did it take you so long to make that choice? Most likely, it took you that long because you wanted to pick out the perfect item. That is the same way you have to be about excellence and about serving God. "Intensely Crave" excellence. "Intensely Crave" to please God. When you do that, you will stop at nothing to give your absolute best!

Here is a KUESTion:

What is **ONE THING** you have wanted more than anything else?

Write your answer here:

Make **Excellence** your Personal **Passion!**

GOTTA HAVE IT!: Here are some cool items. You can only choose one. Circle the one you'd like to have the most!

KNOW YOUR FRIENDS: How well do you know your friends? Try to guess which one your friends will choose, then have them pick their favorite!

Journal Minute

Today's Date: / /

How was your day today?

What was something funny that happened?

What was something bad that happened?

What did you learn from this lesson?

Expectation

Learn to raise your level of self expectation.

Philippians 3:13-14

"...Forgetting the past and looking forward to what lies ahead, I press on to reach the end of the race and receive the heavenly prize for which God, through Christ Jesus, is calling us."

Everyone who runs in a race, or enters a contest, or competes on any team, has one thing in mind...winning the prize. Most everyone wants to be a winner. Nobody really wants to be a loser. Sometimes we do lose though. And if we ever want to win again, we have to **FORGET** about when we lost. Sometimes we win. And if we ever want to win again, we have to also **FORGET** about when we won. If we win a lot, it is easy to get lazy and stop practicing because we think, "We are good, we don't need to practice!" That is when we lose. When Paul wrote this letter to the Philippians, he was trying to teach them an important lesson, **NEVER** look back. Always move forward. Keep going after the prize of pleasing God!

Here is a KUESTion:

Have you ever won at something one time, but lost the next time?

Write your answer here:

EXCELLENCE
always moves
FORWARD!

MOVE FORWARD: Grab a friend. Choose small objects as your game pieces. Spin a coin to see how many spaces you move. Heads = 1, Tails = 2. Only do what the box says if you land on it after a coin spin. First one to finish, wins.

START

FINISH

	BACK 2	AHEAD 2
AHEAD 3	BACK 4	AHEAD 2
DOWN 1	UP 1	
LOSE A TURN	UP 1 RIGHT 2	
UP 2		

Journal Minute

Today's Date:

/	/

How was your day today?

What was something funny that happened?

What was something bad that happened?

What did you learn from this lesson?

2.1 TEAMWORK

Teamwork makes the Dream Work

It's All About Trust

Trust Makes a Team Work

Proverbs 3:5-6

"Trust in the LORD with all your heart and lean not on your own understanding; in all your ways acknowledge him, and he will make your paths straight."

What greater power and knowledge is there to put your trust in than in God? It seems a little funny that we would have to be told by the Bible to "Trust God." But all of creation is built on trust. The grass trusts the clouds for rain. The clouds trust the oceans for water to make the rain. Birds trust trees for seeds to eat. The trees trust the ground for nutrients and water to grow and produce fruit that produces seeds for the birds to eat. Our whole existence is based on trust. At the very heart of all that trust is the one who created it all...God. So when we learn to **TRUST** God, we are learning to trust in ourselves, in others, and in all of his creation as well. As you learn to put your trust in God more and more you will learn to trust others more as well, and that will make your team even stronger.

Here is a KUESTion:

Have you ever had to **TRUST** someone?

Write your answer here:

TRUST is something you **GIVE**

SEE YOU IN THE FALL: Get with a friend and an adult. Have your friend stand behind you, then tell them you are going to fall into their arms and that they need to catch you. Then do the same for them. Have the adult make sure you don't get hurt. Draw a picture of you falling into your friend's arms. Then write down how it felt to have to trust them to catch you.

Journal Minute

Today's Date: | / / |

How was your day today?

What was something funny that happened?

What was something bad that happened?

What did you learn from this lesson?

68

Teamwork makes the Dream Work

It's All About Trust

Trust Makes a Team Work

---

1 Samuel 16:7

"But the LORD said to Samuel, 'Don't judge by his appearance or height, for I have rejected him. The LORD doesn't see things the way you see them. People judge by outward appearance, but the LORD looks at the heart.' "

Vision is so much more than just what we can physically see. Some people are not able to see with their physical eyes, yet they still have vision. Whether we are seeing with our eyes, or our ears, or even with touch, everything is processed by our mind. This is why we can close our eyes, hear a sound and instantly see a picture of what that sound represents in our minds. Sometimes we make decisions about what we think by what we see. We see an old toy and decide we don't want it because it's old. Or we see a brand new toy and decide we'd love to have it because it's shiny and new. But we find out later that the older toy is better than the newer toy. The same thing is true of learning to trust others. Sometimes we look at someone and think we can't trust them, but once we get to know them, we find out we can trust them. Getting to know your team will make your team stronger.

Here is a KUESTion:

Do you find it hard to **TRUST** something you don't **KNOW?**

Write your answer here:

We **TRUST** what we **KNOW!**

70

OH, I SEE: Which of these items do you trust the most? Which do you trust the least? Write them next to the numbers.

- Styrofoam cup with holes
- Piece of moldy bread
- Small plastic chair
- Big, strong chair
- Happy dog
- An angry alligator
- A Police officer
- A plane with no wings
- Fresh hot pizza
- Your friends

I totally trust:

1

2

3

No way I trust:

1

2

3

Journal Minute

Today's Date: | / / |

How was your day today?

What was something funny that happened?

What was something bad that happened?

What did you learn from this lesson?

It's All About Trust

Trust Makes a Team Work

Deuteronomy 7:9

"Know therefore that the LORD your God is God; he is the faithful God, keeping his covenant of love to a thousand generations of those who love him and keep his commands."

God is faithful! He can be trusted! We believe this because He always keeps His Word. When God says "yes", He means, "Yes!" When He says "No," He means "No!" Like the scripture above tells us, He keeps His word to a thousand generations. That would roughly be about 40,000 years!! WOW!! That's a long time to keep your word! It is His commitment to His Word that causes us to be able to trust Him. Doing what you say you will do is a HUGE part of being someone others can trust. If you want others to trust you, simply do what you say! We build our world with our words, and we build trust in others by keeping our word! Think about what you are saying you will do, then when you are committed, say it and do it, and others will always trust you!

Here is a KUESTion:

Can your friends **TRUST** you to do what you **SAY**?

Write your answer here:

I **ALWAYS** keep my WORD!

YOU SAID IT: Below are a bunch of things you might say. If you did, which one would your friends be able to trust you to actually do? Put a star next to those. Now ask a friend and have them put a dot next to the ones they would trust you to do.

"I will pray for you"

"I won't tell anyone!"

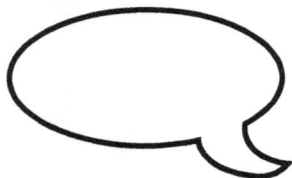

"I'll clean your room for you!"

"You can trust me!"

"You can have all my toys if you win!"

"I will do my best!"

Journal Minute

Today's Date: / /

How was your day today?

What was something funny that happened?

What was something bad that happened?

What did you learn from this lesson?

It's All About Trust

Trust Makes a Team Work

Matthew 18:21

"Then Peter came to him and asked, 'Lord, how often should I forgive someone who sins against me? Seven times?' 'No, not seven times,' Jesus replied, 'but seventy times seven!' "

Sometimes we think that we are only obligated to forgive someone once or twice. They do something that hurts our feelings, or causes us to be upset. We get over it and forgive them. Then they do it again. This time it is a little harder to finally get to where we can forgive them, but we finally do forgive them. Then they do it again! This time is MUCH HARDER to be able to forgive them. But somehow we find a way to forgive them. THEN THEY DO IT AGAIN!! What if they did it 490 times? Would you think we would have to forgive them? Jesus tells us that we should always forgive! He tells Peter to forgive 490 times!! That's a lot! But the point is not the number, it is the attitude to always forgive!

Here is a KUESTion:

Have you ever had to FORGIVE a friend?

Write your answer here:

Forgiving others makes you more TRUSTWORTHY!

VERY FORGIVING: In the puzzle below, find the items that break easily. Think about how forgiving you must be to earn the trust of others:

EGG, GLASS, FLOWER, WATERBALLOON, CRYSTAL, NECKLACE, ICE

```
N R G X P Q D T S O E G Z B W G A L S W E L X W O D R S L F
D E W C W K L S Q P X N W P A C W K N A C O W D K I D N A L
D N C W D J O W C E G G S P U B V E W N I P W E F J N P W O
N C E K I N C W N W E O J V W E C M G C N U T Y W B E U D W
W A T E R B A L O O N Z X J K W S X L N Q P D N Q O F U Y E
F N S O C I C N Q Q W I R F I U Y P A D C N T R P G V D C R
D M W E P O M V V N E P Q P O C R Y S T A L B W J K S M K S
N E C K L A C E N N W J Q O S I J S S W E R O I V B J K L W
```

BREAK THE ICE: Ask a parent for help. Get a piece of ice from your freezer. Wrap it up in a towel and have someone older help you break it. Slowly unwrap the towel and quickly see how many pieces the ice broke into.

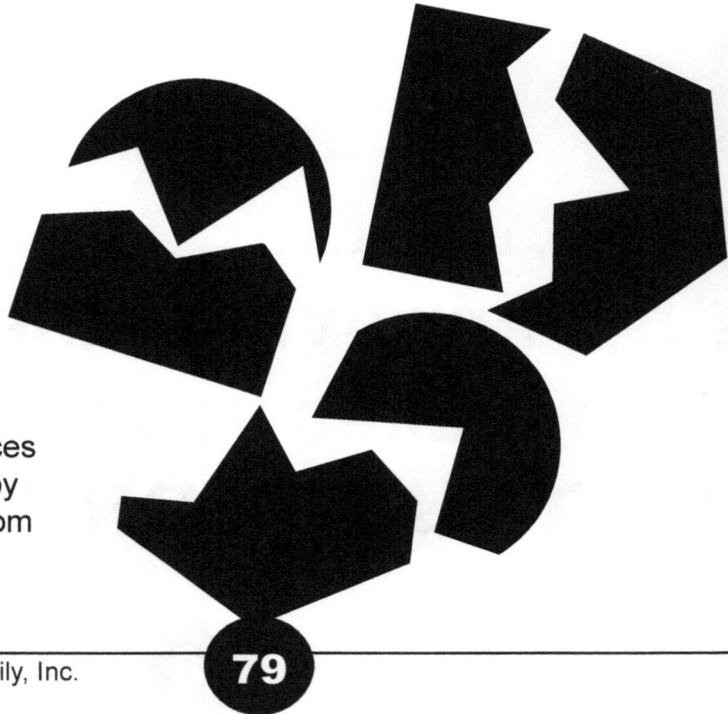

GET IT TOGETHER: Connect the pieces that fit together by drawing a line from one to another.

Journal Minute

Today's Date: | / / |

How was your day today?

What was something funny that happened?

What was something bad that happened?

What did you learn from this lesson?

God is my Authority

Respecting Authority

I am on a SUB-MISSION!

---

1 Peter 5:5

"Young men, in the same way be submissive to those who are older. All of you, clothe yourselves with humility toward one another, because, "God opposes the proud but gives grace to the humble."

Did you know that the only way you can lift something over your head is if you get under it? It is impossible for you to be over something that is over you. I know this sounds simple, but there are a lot of people who believe that, when it comes to following instructions, that they do not have to do what they are asked to do. When it comes to authority, they don't want to be under anybody. They want to be over everyone. But it is impossible to be the servant and the leader at the same time. Even if you are a leader, when you choose to serve someone on the team, you become the servant. You **SUBMIT** yourself to them. That is what it means to be **SUBMISSIVE**, to be under someone's authority.

Here is a KUESTion:

Who is someone that is in authority OVER you?

Write your answer here:

I respect **AUTHORITY** in my life!

SUBMARINE: Put some small rocks in a baggy. Blow up a small balloon. Tie the baggy to the balloon with a string. Fill your sink with water. See if the rocks sink the balloon. Add rocks until it sinks. Now answer these questions:

How many rocks did it take to keep the balloon under water?

☐

Did you think that the rocks could cause the balloon to sink?

YES   NO

How many rocks do you think it would take to sink a ship?

☐

How can you serve better under your leader's authority?

BAGGY SUB: Take a minute to draw a picture of what your baggy sub looks like!

Journal Minute

Today's Date: [/   /   ]

How was your day today?

What was something funny that happened?

What was something bad that happened?

What did you learn from this lesson?

God is my Authority

Respecting Authority

I am on a SUB-MISSION!

Genesis 9:14-15

"When I send clouds over the earth, the rainbow will appear in the clouds, and I will remember my covenant with you and with all living creatures. Never again will the floodwaters destroy all life."

Aren't rainbows cool? They are a sign of peace around the world. Even though rainbows are a sign of peace they are also a sign of authority. Rainbows remind us of one of the most powerfully destructive times in the history of the world, the great flood. God said that every time there is a rainbow in the sky, HE will remember His agreement with mankind to never again flood the earth the way He did in Noah's time. Rainbows cause God to **RESPECT** His promise and rainbows cause us to **RESPECT** God. Whenever you see a rainbow you **REMEMBER** or **RESPECT** what happened in Noah's day and what God promised to all of us - to never flood the earth again. Remembering is a big part of learning to respect authority, even the authority of rainbows.

Here is a KUESTion:

Have you ever seen a really bright **RAINBOW?**

Write your answer here:

I am **observant** and **RESPECTFUL!**

WHAT NEXT? Take a plastic bottle and fill it to the very top with water, then place the cap back on the bottle. Now place the bottle in the freezer overnight. Answer the following questions before and after you put the bottle in the freezer:

BEFORE: (when you put the bottle in the freezer)

> What do you think will happen to the bottle?

> Do you think the water will freeze?

AFTER: (the next day)

> Did anything unusual happen to the bottle?

> Was this unexpected?

Journal Minute

Today's Date: / /

How was your day today?

What was something funny that happened?

What was something bad that happened?

What did you learn from this lesson?

God is my Authority

Respecting Authority

I am on a SUB-MISSION!

Psalms 36:5-7

"Your unfailing love, O LORD, is as vast as the heavens; your faithfulness reaches beyond the clouds. Your righteousness is like the mighty mountains, your justice like the ocean depths. You care for people and animals alike, O LORD. How precious is your unfailing love, O God! All humanity finds shelter in the shadow of your wings. "

Have you ever swam in the ocean? Have you ever stood on a mountain? Have you ever been to the zoo and thought about how BIG elephants are and how powerful lions are? All of those things, mountains, oceans, animals are God's creation! He made them with just His Words! If they are so grand and powerful, how much more powerful must God be to be able to just speak a word and create them all? God is worthy of ALL of our respect!

Here is a KUESTion:

What is the BIGGEST animal you have ever seen up close?

Write your answer here:

God is **POWERFUL** and I am His **SERVANT!**

90

PERSPECTIVE: Draw a picture of a mountain or ocean or the world. Then, make the smallest tiny dot you can with your pen or pencil. Give your dot a name. Using a magnifying glass, look at your dot and see how small it is compared to the drawing that you made. Don't tell your friends where your dot is and see if they can find it.

Journal Minute

Today's Date: | / / |

How was your day today?

What was something funny that happened?

What was something bad that happened?

What did you learn from this lesson?

God is my Authority

Respecting Authority

I am on a SUB-MISSION!

Psalms 1:1-3

"Blessed is the man who does not walk in the counsel of the wicked or stand in the way of sinners or sit in the seat of mockers. But his delight is in the law of the LORD, and on his law he meditates day and night. He is like a tree planted by streams of water, which yields its fruit in season and whose leaf does not wither. Whatever he does prospers."

Who we choose to walk with, where we choose to stand and where we choose to sit can make a big difference in our lives. If we choose to hang out with those friends who are always getting in trouble, then we will get in trouble. If we choose to be around those friends that are always giving bad advice or trying to get us to do stuff we shouldn't do, then we are going to have problems. But if we will choose, even when it's hard, to be around the right people, make the right choices and stay focused on pleasing God, then we will be successful and enjoy a good life!

Here is a KUESTion:

Have you ever held a door open for someone? What did they say?

Write your answer here:

I show **RESPECT** even when I don't feel like it!

PERFECT PRACTICE MAKES PERFECT: Do the following practice exercises then put a check mark in the box once you have completed them. See how soon you can get them done.

☐ Hold a door open for someone.

☐ Look someone in the eye the entire time they are talking to you.

☐ When an older person walks in the room, stand up and say, "Hi, nice to see you!"

☐ The next time your parents ask you to do something, say, "Yes Ma'am (or sir)" and do it right away.

☐ Clean your room BEFORE you are asked to.

☐ The next time you eat with your family or friends, volunteer to be the one who gives thanks for the food.

Journal Minute

Today's Date: / /

How was your day today?

What was something funny that happened?

What was something bad that happened?

What did you learn from this lesson?

Excellence is an Attitude

A More Excellent way

The way of excellence is the way of love.

Matthew 7:24-25

**(24)"Anyone who listens to my teaching and follows it is wise, like a person who builds a house on solid rock.
(25) Though the rain comes in torrents and the floodwaters rise and the winds beat against that house, it won't collapse because it is built on bedrock."**

Have you ever built a sand castle? Can you imagine living in a sand castle? With the first big wave, your whole house would be demolished. Now imagine living in a castle built on the top of a great mountain! What could possibly destroy that castle? In fact, we see pictures of castles around the world that are still standing after hundreds of years. It doesn't matter how hard we work, how excellent we are or how great we might be at a certain job, if **LOVE** is not our foundation, eventually, something will happen that will cause our world to fall apart. Whether it is an argument, not getting our way or being bored with what we are doing, we need **LOVE** to help us stay strong when things get tough!

Here is a KUESTion:

Have you ever had to **LOVE** when it was tough?

Write your answer here:

LOVE is Life's FOUNDATION!

BUILD A FOUNDATION: Use the pattern already started to finish drawing the foundation wall.

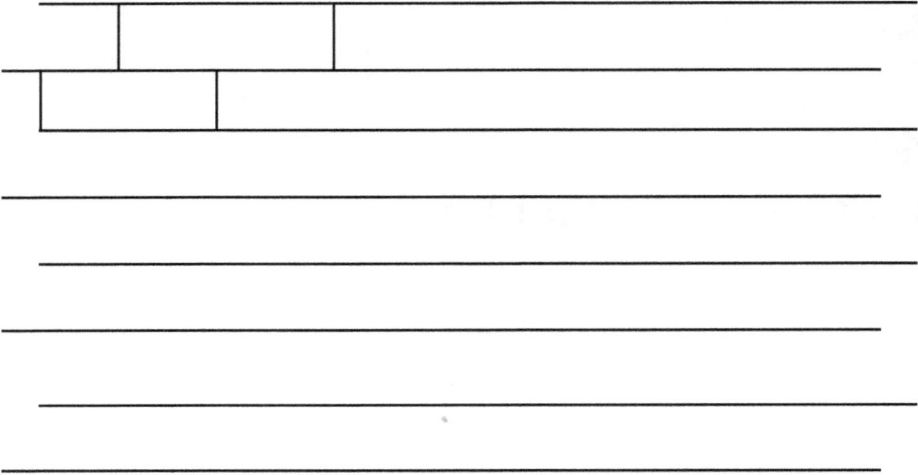

IF YOU BUILD IT: Circle the picture below that would make a solid foundation. If you have these items, try to make a toy stand up on them.

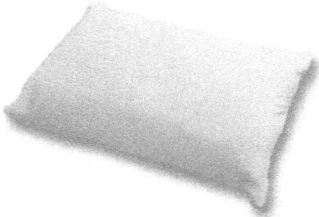

Journal Minute

Today's Date:
/	/

How was your day today?

What was something funny that happened?

What was something bad that happened?

What did you learn from this lesson?

Excellence is an Attitude

A More Excellent way

The way of excellence is the way of love.

1 John 4:16

"And so we know and rely on the love God has for us. God is love. Whoever lives in love lives in God, and God in them."

Isn't it interesting? We talk a lot about doing great things for God, but at the end of it all, the greatest thing God wants from us is the same thing He gives to us...love. In fact, this scripture seems to be telling us something pretty important. That if we are going to live in God, then we must live in love. Our core scripture, 1 Corinthians 13 tells us that **LOVE** is the more excellent way. The gateway to excellence is **LOVE**. The doorway into the excellence building is **LOVE**. The portal into the universe of excellence is **LOVE**. Learning to let love be what motivates you is key to loving God.

The Bible tells us in John 3:16 that God loved us so much that he gave his absolute best for us. He gave up Jesus. Jesus loved us so much that he gave up his very life for us. That is **LOVE**! True love will lead us to living an excellent life of giving our absolute best.

Here is a KUESTion:

Have you ever had to **GIVE** something away that you absolutely **LOVED?**

Write your answer here:

LOVE is something you gain more of when you **GIVE** it away!

THIS IS WHAT I LOVE? Answer the questions below to make a sentence about the things you love!

If I could eat anything in the whole world, I would eat

_____,

and I would eat it with my favorite person in the whole world,

_____,

while we were doing our favorite thing in the whole world,

_____

in our favorite place in the whole world,

_____.

That would be the perfect day!

Journal Minute

Today's Date: [/ /]

How was your day today?

What was something funny that happened?

What was something bad that happened?

What did you learn from this lesson?

Excellence is an Attitude

A More Excellent way

The way of excellence is the way of love.

Philippians 2:3 (MSG)

"Don't push your way to the front; don't sweet-talk your way to the top. Put yourself aside, and help others get ahead. Don't be obsessed with getting your own advantage. Forget yourselves long enough to lend a helping hand."

We often think only of ourselves. We often want what we want when we want it in the way we want it. This often makes us act in selfish ways. We want to make the rules so we can win. We quit playing with a friend because another friend comes along that is doing something more fun. We try to cut in line so that we can be first. Selfishness is the opposite of love, and it will keep us from being excellent. When we learn to love God and love others, it will help us become even more excellent at everything we do. We will straighten chairs, not because we were told to, but because our friend is going to sit there. We will lead worship, not because we are on the team, but because we love God. **LOVE** must become the reason we do what we do, it is the more excellent way.

Here is a KUESTion:

What is something you have done just because you **LOVED** someone?

Write your answer here:

LOVE is the **FUEL** of **EXCELLENCE!**

FINISH THE RACE: All of the cars below are 10 miles from the finish line. The number in front of the car shows how many miles of gas they have left. **1)** Circle the cars that will run out of gas before the finish line. **2)** How can the cars share their gas so that everyone gets to the finish line? Draw a line from one car to another to show who can share gas.

Extra Gas

FINISH

14

7

13

6

Journal Minute

Today's Date: [/ /]

How was your day today?

What was something funny that happened?

What was something bad that happened?

What did you learn from this lesson?

3.4 EXCELLENCE

Excellence is an Attitude

A More Excellent way

The way of excellence is the way of love.

John 13:34-35

"A new command I give you: Love one another. As I have loved you, so you must love one another. By this everyone will know that you are my disciples, if you love one another."

One of the reasons that we have a hard time understanding this scripture is because our world has really messed up what true love is. In fact, popular movies, books, and even lessons that are taught in school have reversed true love. The way our world defines love is all about us. The world's idea of love is about a feeling that we get when we see something we really like. Like our favorite teddy bear or toy, or our favorite food. We say, "I love Teddy!", or "I **LOVE** pizza." We talk about loving those things because of how they make us feel. God's idea of love is not based on what others do for us, or how things make us feel. God's love is simply based on **LOVE** for others. So if you **HATE** straightening chairs, that is because you are being selfish. If you **LOVE** the person who is going to be sitting in that chair, then that **LOVE** will motivate you to straighten it up. The bottom line? **LOVE** is not about you, it is about others.

Here is a KUESTion:

How can you LOVE someone even though they may treat you badly?

Write your answer here:

LOVE is to be GIVEN not GOTTEN!

A HEART CONNECTION: Connect the hearts in numerical order. Now try alphabetical:

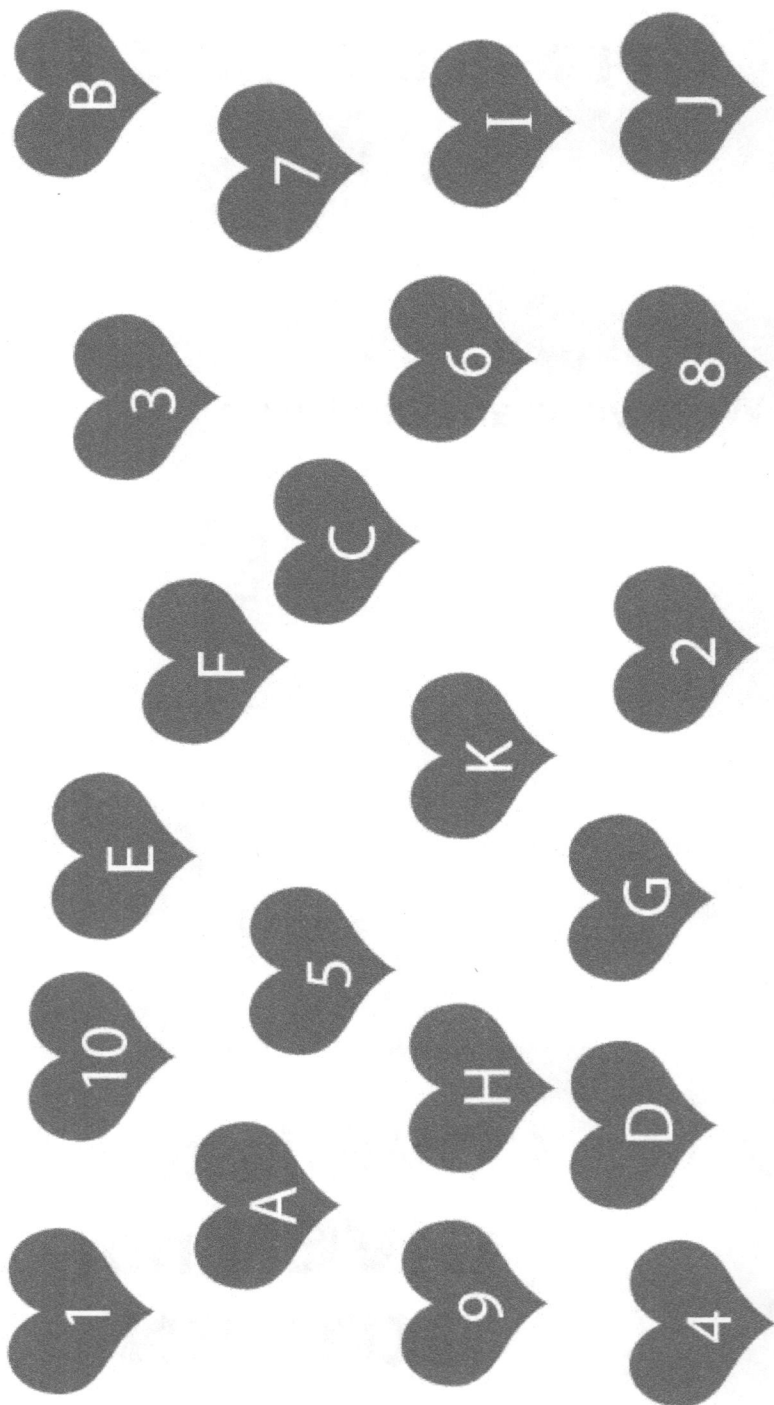

Journal Minute

Today's Date: [/ /]

How was your day today?

What was something funny that happened?

What was something bad that happened?

What did you learn from this lesson?

Eyes on the Prize

I Make the Team's Goal My Goal

Romans 12:4-5

"Just as our bodies have many parts and each part has a special function, so it is with Christ's body. We are many parts of one body, and we all belong to each other."

Have you ever thought about the fact that your hand needs your wrist to do its job? What would it be like if your hand was connected to your elbow? Have you ever thought about the fact that your foot would have a hard time getting anything done without your ankle? We really don't think about our bodies like that very often, but every part of our body depends on other parts to accomplish its job. Imagine trying to turn your head without a neck! In most cases, if you were to take away one part, all the other parts would have to make up for the loss. For example, if you no longer had a knee, your hip and ankle would have to work that much harder for you to get around. The same is true of our team. Every one of us plays a HUGE role in helping others get stuff done. Without every person, we all have to work much harder!

Here is a KUESTion:

Have you ever hurt a **part of your body** that made it hard to get stuff done?

Write your answer here:

"My **TEAM**'s Goal is my **GOAL!**"

114

ALL OUT OF WHACK! Draw a picture of what it would look like if our feet, hands, legs, ears and so on were in different places on our bodies:

Journal Minute

Today's Date: | / | / |

How was your day today?

What was something funny that happened?

What was something bad that happened?

What did you learn from this lesson?

Eyes on the Prize

I Make the Team's Goal My Goal

Luke 18:21-25

" When Jesus heard his answer, he said, ' There is still one thing you haven't done. Sell all your possessions and give the money to the poor, and you will have treasure in heaven. Then come, follow me.' But when the man heard this he became very sad, for he was very rich. "

Sometimes it is very hard to give something up. When something becomes very valuable to us, we often find it hard to let it go. Have you ever had to give up something you liked a lot? When Jesus asked this man to give away his money, he couldn't do it. Jesus knew that this would be an issue if the man joined the team. Many times, when the things we love get in the way of the team, or our own success, we simply need to be willing to let them go.

Here is a KUESTion:

Have you ever had to give something up that you LOVED a lot?

Write your answer here:

I give up my **DREAM** for the **DREAM** of the **TEAM!**

118

GIVE IT UP:
You have fifty pieces of Gold, but your teammates only have a few. How many do you need to give each one so everyone has the same?

$ 50

14

11

7

18

Journal Minute

Today's Date: [/   /   ]

How was your day today?

What was something funny that happened?

What was something bad that happened?

What did you learn from this lesson?

Eyes on the Prize

I Make the Team's Goal My Goal

---

1 Corinthians 2:9

"That is what the Scriptures mean when they say, 'No eye has seen, no ear has heard, and no mind has imagined what God has prepared for those who love him.' "

God has made so many wonderful things. Think of all the stuff he has created that we don't even see every day. Think about how **HUGE** the universe is and how many millions of stars there are that we don't ever ever see, but they are out there! God's plan for us and our team is so **EXPANSIVE** that we may never get to see all of what He has planned for us. But for the part we do know, we must learn to be very focused on getting that job done. Ministering to our friends every week, being excellent in everything we do, giving our absolute best to every job we are given, THAT is being focused! For your team to be its absolute best **EVERY** member of the team must stay focused on the **ONE GOAL** for the day, and for the team. **FOCUS**!

Here is a KUESTion:

What is the ONE JOB you need to FOCUS on for your team?

Write your answer here:

I am FOCUSED on the GOAL!

WHAT IS THAT?: Go to the KUESTKIDS.com
website and click on Journal. Choose "FOCUS" and try to guess what each photo is.

1. _____

2. _____

3. _____

4. _____

5. _____

6. _____

7. _____

8. _____

9. _____

10. _____

Journal Minute

Today's Date: | / / |

How was your day today?

What was something funny that happened?

What was something bad that happened?

What did you learn from this lesson?

124

Eyes on the Prize

I Make the Team's Goal My Goal

Philippians 3:13-14

"Brothers, I do not consider myself yet to have taken hold of it. But one thing I do: Forgetting what is behind and straining toward what is ahead, I press on toward the goal to win the prize for which God has called me heavenward in Christ Jesus."

Paul wrote the book of Philippians, and he tells us that there is only **ONE GOAL** for our lives...pleasing God. In fact, he tells us that he forgets about everything else and gets focused on that **ONE GOAL**. He reminds us that we have to watch to make sure we don't think we have it all together and that we are already perfect. Keeping ourselves focused on pleasing God, remembering we aren't perfect yet, will help us keep pushing to be our best! Inside every one of you is the ability to do better, be better, and think better. Inside you is the ability to be excellent! You have to learn to not accept "good enough", to always push for better. One of the ways you do this is to keep your focus on the prize!

Here is a KUESTion:

What is something you have been **SUCCESSFUL** at doing?

Write your answer here:

SUCCESS is my **ONLY** option!

BULLS-EYE: Using a Dime, spin it and try to get it to land in the Bulls-Eye. Compete against a friend for fun.

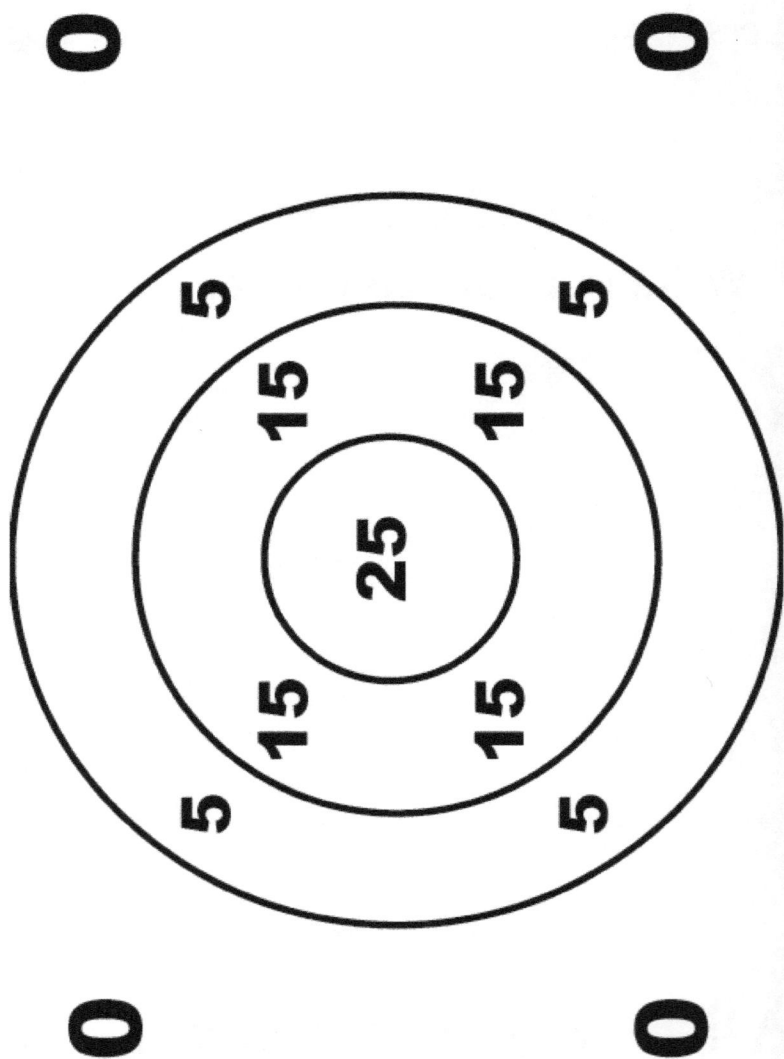

0

0

5

15

15

5

25

15

15

5

5

0

0

Journal Minute

Today's Date: [/   /   ]

How was your day today?

What was something funny that happened?

What was something bad that happened?

What did you learn from this lesson?

God is my Authority

Responding to Authority

I Listen and Obey the First Time!

Joshua 24:15

"But if serving the LORD seems undesirable to you, then choose for yourselves this day whom you will serve...But as for me and my household, we will serve the LORD."

One of the greatest powers that God has given to people is the power of choice. God does not force us to choose to follow Him, it is completely up to us. Joshua refers to this power of choice, and then he tells us the choice he has made for himself and his family. The people he was talking to were having a hard time deciding if they wanted to serve God or to serve other gods and idols. They had not yet recognized God as the **ONE GOD**, and it made it hard for them to decide. But Joshua had already recognized God as the **ONE GOD** so it made his response easy "I will serve **GOD**!" The Bible says that all authority comes from God. When we respond to authority in the right way, obeying our parents, listening to our teachers, obeying laws, following the advice of signs and leaders, we are actually responding to God.

Here is a KUESTion:

How QUICKLY do you respond to the authorities in your life?

Write your answer here:

I RESPOND to what I RECOGNIZE!

130

WATCHA-GONNA-DO?: Read the following
situations then circle what you think you would do:

A friend says a dog is chasing you, should you:

RUN   LAUGH   KEEP WALKING

You find an old can of soda lying in your back yard, should you:

DRINK IT   POUR IT OUT   TASTE IT FIRST

Your mom tells you to clean your room before you go play, but your friends are waiting. Should you:

CLEAN FAST   GO PLAY   MAKE THEM WAIT

Your friend tells you that they stole some money from their dad's wallet. Should you:

NEVER TELL   TELL SOMEONE   MAKE YOUR
FRIEND TELL

You knock over an expensive glass and break it, but your mom thinks it just fell over by itself. Should you:

TELL THE TRUTH   SAY NOTHING   TELL A LIE

Journal Minute

Today's Date: ⟨ / / ⟩

How was your day today?

What was something funny that happened?

What was something bad that happened?

What did you learn from this lesson?

God is my Authority

Responding to Authority

I Listen and Obey the First Time!

John 16:13 (AMP)

"But when He, the Spirit of Truth (the Truth-giving Spirit) comes, He will guide you into all the Truth (the whole, full Truth). For He will not speak His own message [on His own authority]; but He will tell whatever He hears [from the Father..."

Jesus promised to send us the Holy Spirit to live in us and to lead us into truth. The only thing the Holy Spirit says is exactly what He hears the Father say. He never says anything that is just his idea. He says word for word what God the Father is saying. He "echoes" what He hears the Father say. This is the same thing we need to learn to do with those who are in authority over us, including God. What does God say about your life? What does He say about your gifts and talents? What does He say about your future? (read Jeremiah 29:11, Colossians 3:23). This then is what we should be echoing back with our words, with our actions and with our lives.

Here is a KUESTion:

What does God say about the GIFTS He has given you?

Write your answer here:

I say **EXACTLY** what God says about me!

134

FIND THE ECHO: Circle the pictures that are exactly the same.

Journal Minute

Today's Date: [/   /   ]

How was your day today?

What was something funny that happened?

What was something bad that happened?

What did you learn from this lesson?

3.3 AUTHORITY

God is my Authority

Responding to Authority

I Listen and Obey the First Time!

2 Timothy 4:2

"Preach the Word; be prepared in season and out of season; correct, rebuke and encourage—with great patience and careful instruction."

Do your parents ever tell you to "hurry and get ready!" or, "come on, we have to go now or we're going to be late!"? When the time comes for you to leave, that is not the time to still be putting on your shoes, doing your hair, brushing your teeth, or eating a snack. The Bible tells us that we need to **BE READY ALL THE TIME!** Learning to respond to authority the first time is just practice for always being ready. When God calls you to work it's not time to think about it, plan it or figure out whether or not you can; it is time to respond! This is exactly how we should respond to those who are in authority in our lives, as quickly as possible. When our teachers, our parents, our coaches and so on ask us to do something, we should respond as quickly as possible.

© 2019 - CurrentFamily, Inc.

137

Here is a KUESTion:

How **QUICKLY** do you respond to those in authority over you?

Write your answer here:

Excellence **RESPONDS** as quickly as possible!

GET THERE: Find your way to the end of the maze as quickly as possible.

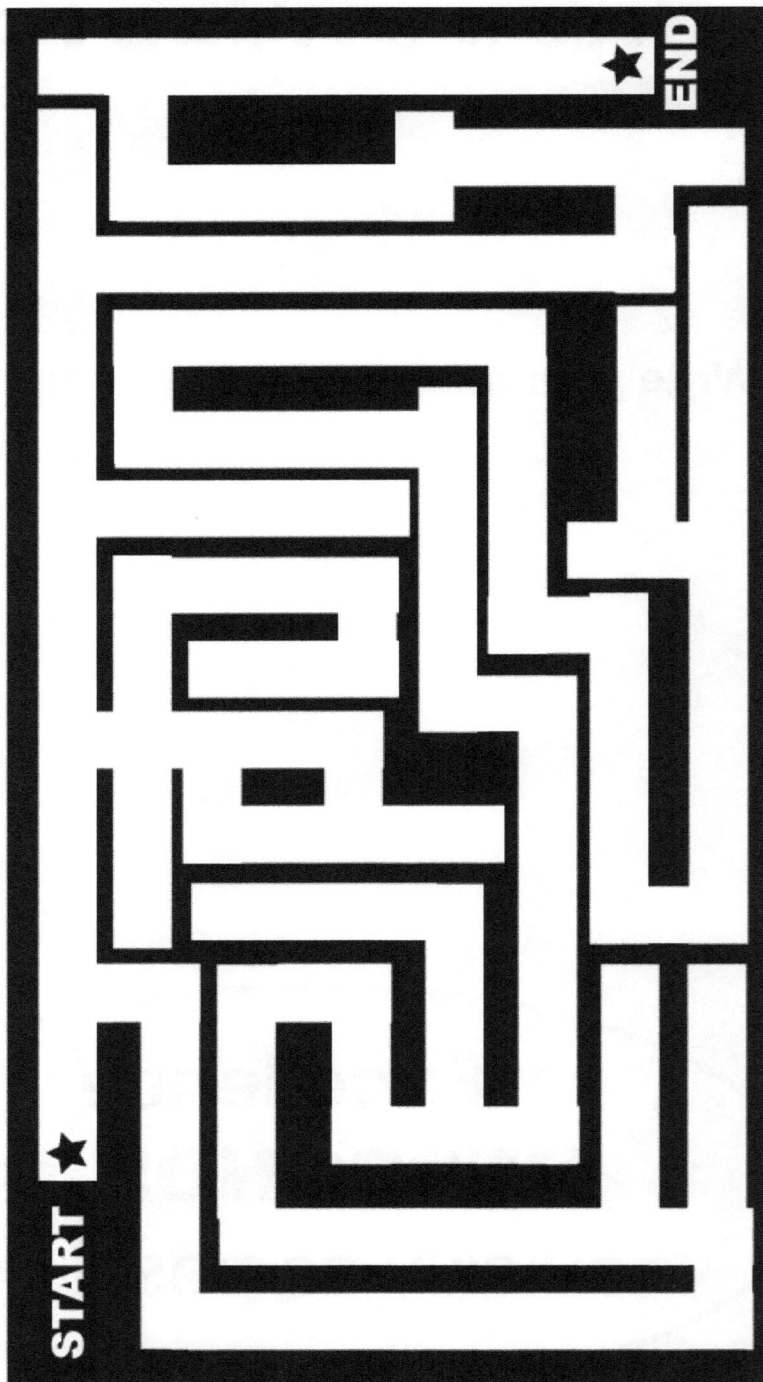

START ★

END ★

139

Journal Minute

Today's Date: | / / |

How was your day today?

What was something funny that happened?

What was something bad that happened?

What did you learn from this lesson?

God is my Authority

Responding to Authority

I Listen and Obey the First Time!

Colossians 3:22

"Slaves, obey your earthly masters in everything; and do it, not only when their eye is on you and to win their favor, but with sincerity of heart and reverence for the Lord."

There is never really a good reason to not give your best. Even when you have limited time or tools, you can still do your absolute best with what you have. Make the most of your time. Make the most of your tools. Make the most of your life. Remembering that what we do with our lives is our response to God's authority in our lives. The Bible reminds us to do everything with all our heart! God cares about us, He has a plan for us, and our response to His authority in our lives is always to be our excellent best! God rewards those who follow Him and serve Him with all their heart. Those kids who serve God with their absolute best, all the time, are the ones He rewards. Remember that God does not want to punish us, He wants to reward us. This should help us when we are asked to give our best. We can get excited about serving God, about giving our best and about responding to His authority in our lives.

141

Here is a KUESTion:

What is the BEST reward you have ever gotten for doing your BEST?

Write your answer here:

I walk by **FAITH** and give my **BEST!**

BULLS-EYE: Wad a small piece of paper into a ball. From about six inches, give yourself ten tries and see how many times you can land in the circle. Then use the charts to see how you score. Have your friends try it as well.

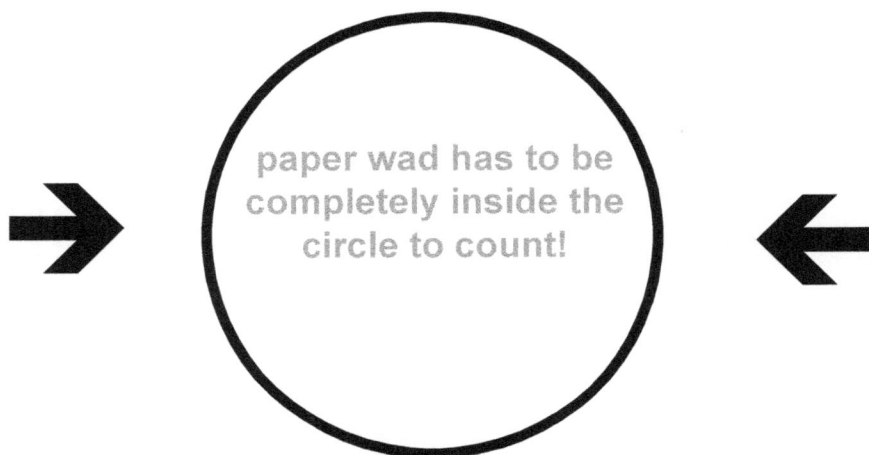

→ paper wad has to be completely inside the circle to count! ←

9-10: Pro Paper Thrower

7-8: Terrific Tosser

5-6: Graceful Goober

3-4: Clumsy Wumsy

1-2: Thumbs McGee

0: BUZZZ!!!

Journal Minute

Today's Date: [/   /   ]

How was your day today?

What was something funny that happened?

What was something bad that happened?

What did you learn from this lesson?